Feng Shui
for Cats

Feng Shui
for Cats

Illustrated by Chris Riddell

Text by Louise Howard

EBURY PRESS
LONDON

First published in 1997

3 5 7 9 10 8 6 4

Text copyright © Louise Howard 1997
Illustrations copyright © Chris Riddell 1997

Chris Riddell has asserted his right to be identified as illustrator of this work.

First published in the United Kingdom in 1997 by Ebury Press
Random House · 20 Vauxhall Bridge Road · London SW1V 2SA

Random House Australia (Pty) Limited
20 Alfred Street · Milsons Point · Sydney · New South Wales 2061 · Australia

Random House New Zealand Limited
18 Poland Road · Glenfield · Auckland 10 · New Zealand

Random House South Africa (Pty) Limited
Endulini · 5a Jubilee Road · Parktown 2193 · South Africa

Random House UK Limited Reg. No. 954009

A CIP catalogue record for this book is available from the British Library

ISBN 0 09 185421 0

Designed by Martin Lovelock

Printed and bound in Great Britain by Mackays of Chatham plc, Kent

Contents

Chi

Chi is energy or force

The chi of the young is very unstable

Chi can flow up ...

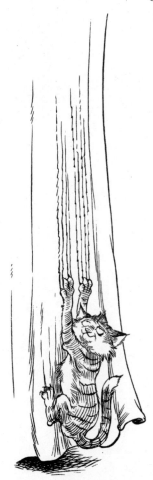

... or down

Yellow, brown or bare patches on the lawn
indicate unhealthy chi

Chi rushes out of a badly placed door or window

A bubbling fish tank may help to circulate new chi

For good chi install bells or lights to
go on when doors are opened

Yang is active

Yin is passive

Yin and yang depend upon each other

Water fountains make for positive chi

When knitting, receive blessings for good chi

Chi arises and vanishes in a cycle

A bed facing east catches the most positive cosmic flow

A mirror in a confined entrance
helps chi to circulate more freely

Harmony

The principle of balance is essential to feng shui

Searching for balance, we stumble upon feng shui

The size of doors is all-important

Place a plant in any unbalanced spot

A poorly designed residence is ...

... to be avoided

Follow the natural rhythms of nature

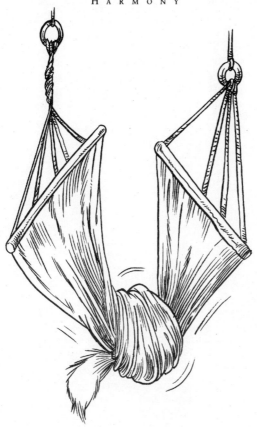

Balance and equilibrium restore harmony
with the environment

Small crystal balls can resolve imbalance

An unbalanced entrance can be a serious problem

Relationships

Relationships are perpetually in flux …

... yet cyclical

A cleverly placed mirror can restore
a problem relationship

To help revive a stagnant relationship, try mirrors,
windmills, mobiles, whirligigs and chimes

To help a difficult relationship,
try moving the bed a few inches to one side

It is stressful for an underling to have
to sit directly opposite his superior

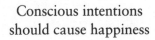

Conscious intentions
should cause happiness

Clutter in the relationship area
can cause disagreements

Health

For good health, find a dwelling with a view of water

An over-large pond is weakening

A cat with thick shining fur indicates good health

Any size of mirror will do to attract good health

A confined space will debilitate your health

A beaded curtain can
relieve an unhealthy view

Overindulgence destroys equilibrium

One's position in space affects one's health

Prosperity

Fish enrich any home

Lucky shapes have meaning and should balance

Observe future neighbours for signs
of prosperity or ill fortune

Ponds should be well stocked with fish

If your lavatory is in the wealth area of your house
you may flush good fortune away

Toads symbolise wealth

Fish absorb accidents and general bad luck

Particular places are luckier ...

... than others

A favourite chair should always face the entrance

Correct feng shui ensures a lifetime of good fortune